# the lanyard book

## Arlene Hamilton Stewart

A Smallwood & Stewart Book

Andrews and McMeel
A Universal Press Syndicate Company

*For my wonderful daughter Annalee Levine,*
*whose dedication made this book possible.*

ISBN: 0-8362-4223-8

Book printed in Hong Kong
Box printed in Hong Kong
Components and plastic box made in China

First U.S. edition
3  5  7  9  10  8  6  4  2

Design   Carol Bokuniewicz Design
Photography   Ross Whitaker
Styling   Maria McBride-Mellinger
Illustrations   Debra Ziss
PRODUCED BY SMALLWOOD AND STEWART, INC.
NEW YORK CITY

ATTENTION: SCHOOLS AND BUSINESSES
Andrews and McMeel books are available at quantity
discounts with bulk purchase for educational, business,
or sales promotional use. For more information, please
write: Special Sales Department, Andrews and McMeel,
4900 Main Street, Kansas City, Missouri 64112.

# contents

## beginner:

## intermediate:

## advanced:

## super advanced:

# introduction

When people think about lanyards they imagine lifeguards swinging whistles on colorful braided rope. The lifeguard lanyard is a classic, but today kids take lanyard laces and create things of beauty with them, like friendship bracelets and necklaces, key rings, sunglass holders, hair ornaments, and many others.

## Where do lanyards come from?

Lanyard making, or as some would call it, "fancy knotting," is a fine old folk art that was developed by young sailors in the days before jet planes. Stuck out at sea for months at end, with no VCRs or portable headsets in sight, sailors took discarded rope from old riggings and started making intricate knots and patterns. Their deft knotting and interlacing turned something ordinary into something special, much as kids have done today with plastic laces.

## What are lanyards today?

Young children may not ship out to sea anymore, but they have found lots of exciting ways to bring lanyard making into the 1990s. Nowadays, plastic laces are the most popular material, but great things can be made with leather, string, even rope. Every project, every stitch we show is portable, needing no more than your hands, and perhaps small scissors or a pocket knife to finish. Best of all, you can do your stitching by yourself, anywhere— on the school bus, on vacation, on long car rides, on plane trips, or on rainy days.

# The basic stitches are easy.

And once you get the hang of it, it's hard to stop! You can make terrific projects from even the most basic stitches and you can add on beads or charms or create your own designs. One of the things that's great about learning is that you can pull out your work and start all over if you want to change it. We've included a variety of stitches from basic to advanced so you can always move up.

# "If at first you don't succeed . . . "

Remember, your stitches will improve each time you practice. Most of the stitches are simple, and we've written the instructions clearly so that even Mom and Dad can help you, if necessary.

# Go for it!

We've supplied you with enough laces to make a range of the stitches and projects here. Don't forget, the laces can be used over and over again until you've nailed down a stitch. If you need more supplies, look for a crafts store near you and stock up on laces so that you can continue making exciting stitches and projects.

# before you begin...

This kit contains enough laces to make the Classic Lanyard or any number of other fun projects: key chains, bike streamers, bracelets, and more.

## Take a minute to look at the:

- plastic laces
- lanyard clips
- key rings
- pony beads

All the instructions are written for right-handed kids. If you're a lefty, just reverse them.

Some kids find it easier to make stitches if the laces are cut on the diagonal. Just snip the ends on a slant before starting, then see if it works better for you.

## remember:

With all the stitches, keep your laces **flat**—don't allow them to twist. For a smooth, uniform look, the secret to success is always pulling the laces **tight** after each stitch—unless the instructions tell you not to.

To make the directions easier to follow, we've illustrated all the stitches in contrasting light and dark colors. When you're learning the stitches, try to use dark and light colors, too. Some of the stitches are harder to do than others—don't panic. The great thing about lanyard making is that you can take out your work and start over!

# the zipper stitch

**The easiest stitch of all! Woven with two or more colors, it actually looks like a zipper.**

Zipper

## to start:

Take three equal length strands. We're using two dark and one light. Make a simple knot as shown.

**1.** Pick up the light lace on the left. Braid **over** the middle lace, **under** the outside right lace. Pull tight.

**Want an "open" zipper? Hold one end in each hand, simply pull. To "close," push in from both ends.**

**tip:**
always keep your "working lace" flat to maintain the Zipper design.

**2.** Now reverse the direction of the light lace and thread **over** the right dark lace and **under** the left lace. Pull tight, pushing up on the lace to make zipper "teeth."

**3.** Repeat "over/under," pulling tight after each stitch, until your Zipper is as long as you want it.

**4.** **To end:** Weave the light strand into the last few stitches of light lace on the back of the zipper. Tie dark laces in a knot if you want.

# chinese staircase

## simple staircase

**Do it in one color or do it in twenty. Master the basics of this simple stitch, then move on to its many fabulous variations.**

## to start:

It's best to learn this stitch with different colors. We'll use dark and light to illustrate. Take three equal lengths. Make an overhand knot at the end. Note: You will see only one color in a completed simple Chinese Staircase.

**1.** Wrap the light lace on the left side over the two dark laces.

**2.** Now, loop the same light lace around the **back** of the two dark loops and insert it through the loop you made on the left and pull **all** the way through. Be careful not to twist the laces. Pull tight.

**3.** Repeat the stitch, always using the **outside** left lace to make your loop. This creates the spiral. About ten stitches make a spiral.

**4.** To end, pull tight on the last stitch. Cut the strands as short as you want.

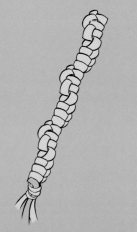

# chinese

## staircase

**beginner**

## multi-color chinese staircase

For a three-color Chinese Staircase, start with three strands of lace, each a different color. Follow the instructions for the simple Staircase, keeping one lace on the outside for as many stitches as you want.

Usually, it is best to wait until one spiral (about ten stitches) has been completed. Then, to introduce a new color, take one of the other two laces and do ten stitches. Then pick up the last color. Repeat.

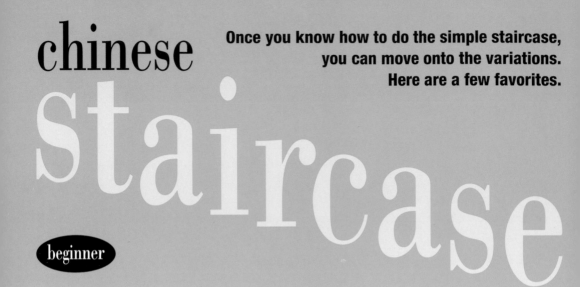

# super staircase

If you want to make a thick Chinese Staircase with many colors , start with lots of colored laces. Count your stitches before changing colors—switch laces when you have the same number of stitches in each spiral.

double helix

Take three strands of one color lace and three strands of another color. Make a knot at the top, Divide into two sections: three on one side and three on the other. Take the outside lace of one color and, going around the other laces of the same color, do the Chinese Staircase stitch. Repeat until you have ten stitches.

Then take the three strands of the other color of lace and make a Chinese Staircase using the left lace to wrap around the other two of that color. Do this until you have ten stitches. Then take one lace of the first color and, going around the other five laces,

make a Chinese Staircase.

Then divide strands back into threes. Reverse colors and continue making separate Staircases—one on the left, one on the right. Bring them back together again and lace a new spiral to match your pattern. Keep going!

double helix

15

The Box Stitch is one of the most popular basic stitches. And, once you've learned the Box Start you can use it for the Box, the Barrel, and the Cobra stitches.

# the box start

**1.** Cross two equal length laces over one another. Hold between your thumb and index finger.

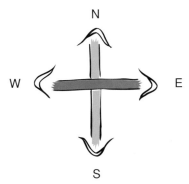

**2.** With your free hand, loop the North lace DOWN and the South lace UP.

Loop laces around the back of your index finger and hold in place.

**3.** Then, pick up the East lace and go **over** the loop you just made with the South lace, and **under** the North lace.

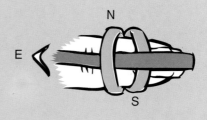

**4.** Now, take the West lace, pull it up from behind your finger, loop it **over** the North lace, **under** the South. Pull all four laces tight. You've got a Box—now you have started!

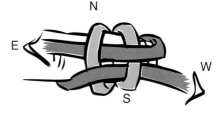

# now, add on the box stitches.

Thread the West lace **over** the South loop, **under** the North.

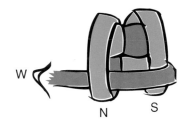

1. With the "four corners" side face up take the North and South laces, just as you did for the Start, loop the North **up,** the South **down.** Hold with your finger.

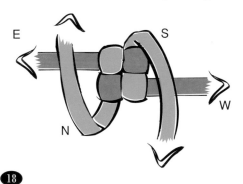

3. Finally, thread the East lace **over** the North lace and **under** the South. **Pull all laces tight.**

**5.** **To end:** Leave yourself about two inches of lace to work with. You can either:

**a.** Drape East and West laces across the box, then tie a simple knot between North and South to secure. . . .

**4.** Continue making the Box Stitch until it's as long as you want.

**b.** . . . or tie an overhand knot on the end of each lace.

# the butterfly

As spectacular as its name implies, the Butterfly looks harder than it is. This is a terrific stitch to use when you want a special braided effect. It looks especially good in bright contrasting colors.

1. Cut off two strands of equal length. Make a slip knot with the light lace: Starting about three inches down, make a simple circle at its end (as shown.) Holding it in your right hand, push the left (longer) end up inside the loop. Pull the first loop tight.

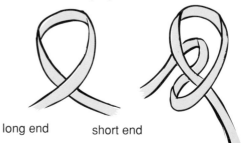

long end          short end

**2.** Make a loop about three inches down from the top of your dark lace, place it inside the slip knot you made with the light lace. Now close up the light loop by pulling tight on the long light lace.

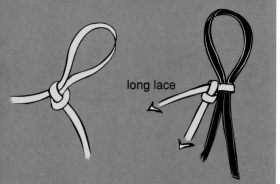

long lace

**3.** To create the Butterfly pattern, loop the **light** lace through your new **dark** loop. Pull dark laces to secure.

**4.** Repeat stitch by making loops with the long dark lace, then the long light lace. Continue until the Butterfly is as long as you want it.

**5.** **To finish:** Instead of making a new loop with your lace, thread the lace through the last loop and pull tight.

# careful!

**It looks just like a real cobra. You can make it with two colors, four colors, or just one.**

*the cobra stitch*

**1.** Use the start for the Box Stitch. Then, take the light lace and dark lace on the bottom and keep them in the middle by holding them between your left thumb and index finger. These are your "middle laces."

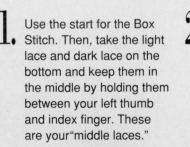

middle laces

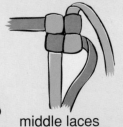

**2.** Move the light lace on the top **over** the two middle laces. Put on the left side. Hold in place.

**3.** Wrap the dark lace from the left side **over** the light lace you just used, then **under** the middle laces.

**4.** Loop this same dark lace up through the light lace on the right and pull the laces tight. Turn over.

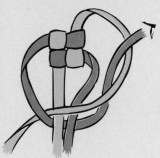

**5.** Move the left dark lace **over** the middle laces.

**6.** Then thread the light lace **over** the dark lace on the right and **behind** the two middle laces.

**7.** Pull the light lace up through the dark loop. Now pull tight with both hands. This is your first stitch. Turn over.

**8.** Repeat Steps 2 through 7. Keep going for as long as you want, then try the endings on the next pages.

**tip:**

you can always tell which strand goes in front because it's the color of the middle stripe.

# then the finish:

**Separate the dark stitches from the light. Pull tight. Tie all four laces in an overhand knot, or . . .**

*make a fabulous cobra head*

1. Turn the Cobra upside down to reverse the direction you're working in—as shown—to make the head.

2. Separate the laces by pulling one on the outside left, one on the right. The two middle laces will be used later for "fangs."

**3.** Do the simple Cobra Stitch for about six stitches. The only difference is that instead of going over and under laces, you are going over and under the body of the Cobra. Pull tight. If you want to make a really "fat" head, reverse direction after six stitches, then repeat stitches.

**4.** End your stitch at the top of the Cobra Head.

**5.** Cut the "fangs" to the length you want.

**6.** Take the remaining two laces, knot in back, then cut really short.

advanced

Smooth
and precise,
the Diamond is a
beautiful round stitch.
It's very intricate but well
worth learning because it's the
stitch used for the Classic Lanyard.
It's also great for friendship
bracelets. Use it anytime
you want to impress
people with
your skill.

# the diamond

# to start:

Fold two equal length laces over. Make an overhand knot in the middle. Now you have four equal strands. We're going to label these laces 1, 2, 3, and 4.

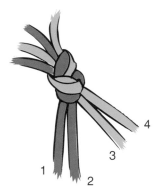

**1.** Pick up lace #4, bring it **under** #2 and 3, then wrap **over** #2.

**2.** Bring lace #1 **under** both lace #2 and #4. Now, wrap #1 **over** the front of lace #4, bringing it out to the left side as shown. Pull all the laces tight (the stitch may seem loose). This is your pattern. Keep going.

**3.** Always taking the outside lace to weave around the two inside, repeat Steps 1 and 2 until your Diamond is as long as you want it. To end, make a simple knot in two laces.

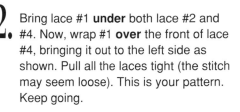

# the barrel

Also known as the Round Stitch, the Barrel Stitch has a tight, dynamic texture. Because this stitch is round, you have to be extra careful where you put your laces. With a little practice, soon you'll have a great barber pole look.

advanced

## to start:

Cut two strands of lace the same length. Then follow the instructions for the Box Start (see page 16).

1. Put the "four corners" side face up. Now take the top right (light) lace and bring it down **flat** against the side of the bottom left quarter.

**2.** Bring **up** the bottom left strand and place that flat against the top right quarter stitch. Hold both these stitches with your fingers.

**4.** Pick up the last strand from the top left, go **over** the first light loop then through the bottom right stitch. Pull tight. Here's your first stitch.

**3.** Now, weave the bottom right quarter strand **over** the first light loop, **under** the second, ending at the top. Place flat against the top.

**5.** Keep repeating from Step 1. When done, tie the strands together or tie each lace in a separate knot.

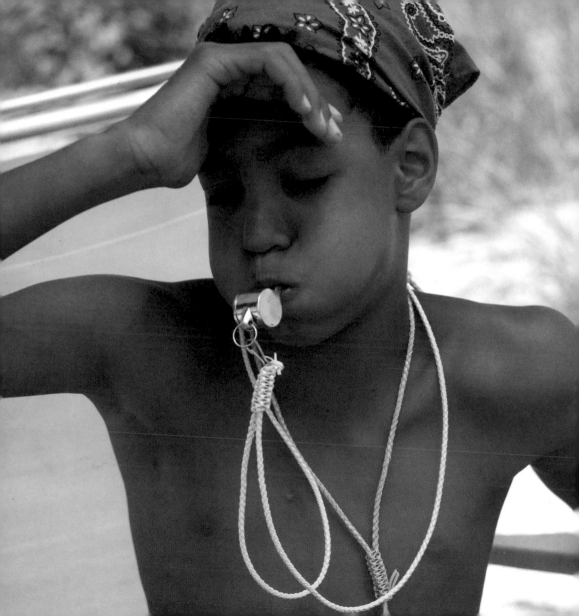

# the big box

**Fat and fun, this requires patience—it's worth it! You can go on to make some amazing projects. Soon you'll be creating your own Big Box with as many laces as you can handle.**

## to start:

Take four equal length laces, lay out as shown.

1. Wrap laces between your index finger and thumb.

2. Starting from right: Loop yellow lace #4 down, and #3 up. Do the same thing with the reds.

3. Take top blue from left side. Go over first red lace, under second red lace, over first yellow, under second yellow.

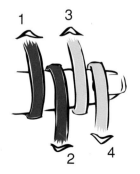

**4.** Take blue on right side. Go over lace #4, under #3, over #2, under #1.

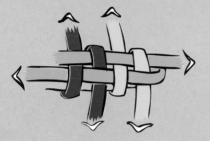

**5.** Take green lace from left bottom. Go over #1, under #2, over #3, under #4.

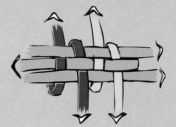

**6.** Take green lace from bottom right. Go over #4, under #3, over #2, under #1. **Pull all laces tight.**

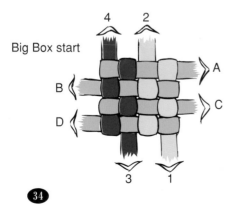

Big Box start

**7.** Note: Lace numbers have changed, as shown in the illustration. Loop lace #1 over top. Loop lace #2 down. Take lace #3, loop up. Take #4, loop down.

**8.** From the right side, take Lace A. Go over #1, under #2, over #3, under #4.

**10.** Take lace C from right. Go over #1, under #2, over #3, under #4.

**9.** From the left take lace B. Go over #4, under #3, over #2, under #1.

**11.** Take lace D from left. Go over #4, under #3, over #2, under #1. Pull tight. This starts the stitching.

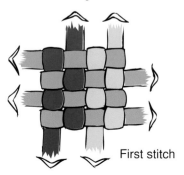

First stitch

**12.** To continue the pattern, always loop laces 1 and 2 up and down, then follow the pattern with the other laces.

**To end:** Turn upside down. Do a Chinese Staircase with one color for at least six stitches.

# the big

**Fabulous! Tricky, but goes fast once you get the hang of it. Use this for a more complex design such as the Scrambler.**

1. Use the same start as the Big Box with as many laces in whatever colors you want. (Don't pull stitches too tight.)

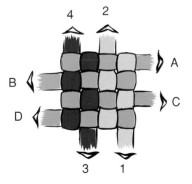

# barrel

**2.** Take #1. Bring over to lay flat on the left side of #2.

**3.** Take #2 and loop it down to the right side of #1. Hold with your fingers.

**4.** Take #3 and loop to the left of #4. Loop #4 down to the right of #3.

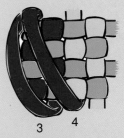

**5.** Take lace B from left side. Go over #3, under #4, over #1, under #2.

**6.** Take lace A. Go over #2, under #1, over #4, and under #3.

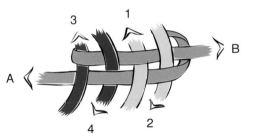

**7.** Take lace D. Go over #3, under #4, over #1, under #2.

**8.** Take lace C. Go over #2, under #1, over #4, under #3.

**9.** Pull closed. Repeat Steps 2 to 9 for pattern. Use same ending as for the Big Box.

**Super advanced
and super fabulous!
Build it upon the
Big Box and
the Big Barrel.**

# the scrambler

**1.** Take four lengths of different colors about two yards long each. Fold in half. Use the same start as you did for the Big Box. Attach a key ring now if you want one.

**2.** Do ten stitches of the Big Barrel.

**3.** Then do one stitch of the Big Box.

**4.** Repeat Steps 2 and 3 until Scrambler is desired length.

**5.** End as you would for the Big Box.

projects

Is anything cooler? Every lifeguard has one. Here's how to make the authentic lanyard with its trademark slide for the whistle. Use any round stitch you want. We show it as a Diamond Stitch topped off with the Box.

## you need:

- one lanyard clip
- 2 pieces of lace: 3½ yards each for a short lanyard; 4 yards for a long, adult size.
- one whistle

# the
# classic
# lanyard

# the classic lanyard

**1.** Pull the two pieces of lace through the end of the lanyard clip. Make sure your ends are even.

Below is the start for the Diamond Stitch. Follow instructions on pages 26 and 27 or refer to illustrations.
Continue working until you have about 12 inches of lace left.

**2.** To set up for the Box: Tie your laces as illustrated so the light strands face each other and dark strands face each other in opposite directions.

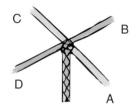

**3.** Take the lower right light lace A, and fold it over, leaving a loop in the end. Now, bring lace B over A.

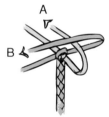

**4.** Fold the light lace C **over** the dark lace D, inside lace B.

**5.** Bring the dark lace D **over** light lace C and into the loop made by light lace A. **Keep all your laces loose for now.**

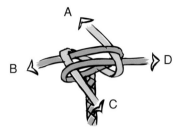

**6.** You should have an open box on top. Take the other end of the Diamond Stitch length and double it through the open box. Loosen up the strands to let the lanyard hook pass through, then tighten. This will create the lanyard slide. Keep stitches loose, so you can slide the lanyard.

**7.** Continue to braid the four laces to make a Box that's about two inches long. Tighten up on the strands but still allow enough slack for the lanyard to slide.

**8.** To end the lanyard: Take light lace A, swing it **under** dark lace B, then insert under C and up through the center of the Box. Don't pull tight yet. Repeat for laces B, C, and D.

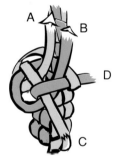

**9.** Now, you can tighten. Pull lace A, then B, C, and D. Trim the ends on a slant. Attach a whistle to the clip and you're ready to roll!

# bike
## streamers

**Bike grips look great streaming with neon colors in the hot Cobra Stitch.**

**The Chinese Staircase would be cool here, too.**

You'll need two bike grips—make sure you get the kind with small holes in the end so you can attach the streamers.

1. Take as many strands as you want in one, two, or more colors. You can make streamers any length. We started with ten strands that were two feet long.

**tip:**
if your slip knot feels sluggish, loosen the lace holding the bundle of laces to the grip and feed it down into the hole. This will pull up on the slip knot.

2. To attach the laces to the bike grip: Take a lace and cut the tips on the diagonal to make your work easier. Thread one end through the hole on the grip. Pull it out and make a simple slip knot (see the Butterfly Stitch, pages 20-21, for instructions).

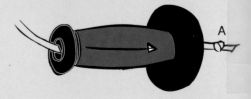
A

**3.** This is "grip" lace A. Leave it dangling. Now, pick up your strands, double them over, and loop your "grip" lace over them, then insert the "grip" lace back through the handle, pushing it all the way in until it comes out the other end. We'll call this lace B.

**4.** Tie the group of strands on the top of the bike grip in a simple knot. Insert lace B into the slip knot. Pull until the slip knot reaches the top on the inside. Make sure it's tight.

**5.** Cut off the dangling end of lace B. Don't worry about still seeing this lace. It will disappear when you put the grips on your bike handlebars. Loosen the top knot and do whatever stitch you like with the group of strands. We used the Cobra to get a wide braided look, stitching for about three inches. Always end with a knot.

One of the best ways to keep your glasses—and your cool! Here it is in the classic Butterfly Stitch. The Barrel or Diamond would work, too. This makes a great gift for your parents or grandparents.

## you need:

- sunglasses
- 2 small ponytail elastics or rubber bands
- 2 strands of lace, each 2½ feet long

The Butterfly Stitch shown is 15 inches long. If you want yours longer, start with 3-foot lengths of lace.

# sunglass hold

1. Take the laces and tie them with a simple knot at one end. Keep it loose. Slip an elastic halfway through the knot opening. Then pull the knot tight.

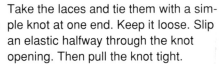

**2.** Start your stitch. When it's as long as you want, leave about three inches of lace at the end. Take the strands, make a knot, slip in the other elastic, pull the knot tight. Knot once more.

**3.** Slip one end over each ear piece. Twist the elastic around until it's tight.

# hair

## ornaments

Great for gifts, and for yourself. You can make fabulous barrettes and headbands in lots of different colors and stitches. For variety, make them multi-color—or in a solid color to match a special outfit.

## solid color barrette
## you need:

- one 4-inch barrette
- one yard of lace

**1.** Divide the lace in half. Loop under the fastener lip.

If you are using the Cobra Stitch, with the front of barrette facing you, take the left lace and loop in front of barrette.

**tip:**
always keep your stitches flat and even in the back to make closing the barrette easier.

From the right side, take lace #1, put over lace #2 then bring it in the back of the barrette and out through the loop on the left side. Pull tight.

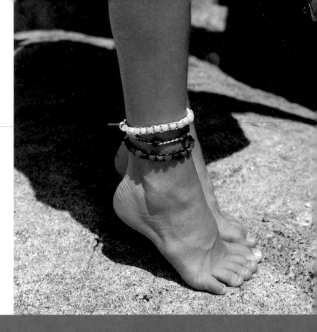

**3.** Take the right end of your lace and slip it through the new bead on the left.

**4.** Pull both ends of lace to prevent beads from slipping, but do not tighten too much. Continue to add beads from the left, slipping right lace through until the bracelet is as long as you want it.

**5.** To end, go back to the first bead, thread ends of laces into this bead in opposite directions. When you pull the laces out, the bracelet will be joined. Tie an overhand knot at the end of each lace as close as possible to the bead.

## Acknowledgements

Thanks to my daughter, Annalee Levine, and to her friends Jana Johnson, Danielle Brown, and Camille Czerkowicz for all their hard work.

Many thanks to an inspiring lanyard maker, Tanya Kukucka.

Smallwood and Stewart would like to thank all the models who did such a fantastic job:

Danielle Brown
Quinn English
Thor Fister
Madeline Hunnewell
Peter Hunnewell
Jana Johnson
Karleigh Kjelberg
Annalee Levine
Antonia O'Donoghue
Ashley O'Donoghue
Courtney Robinson